P9-DEB-177

FOLK TALES FROM THE SOVIET UNION

Compiled by **R. Babloyan** and **M. Shumskaya**
Designed by **M. Anikst**

FOLK TALES FROM THE SOVIET UNION

THE CAUCASUS

RADUGA PUBLISHERS
MOSCOW

CONTENTS

© Raduga Publishers 1987. Illustrated

ISBN 5-05-001559-6
ISBN 5-05-001563-4

GEORGIAN FOLK TALES

The Poor Man and the Knight's Three Pomegranates
    Retold by *Nina Dolidze*
    Translated by *K. M. Cook*
    Illustrations by *Natalia Nesterova*

The Fair Maid From Faraway Nigozeti
    Retold by *Elena Virsaladze*
    Translated by *K. M. Cook*
    Illustrations by *Tengiz Samsonidze*

THE POOR MAN AND THE KNIGHT'S THREE POMEGRANATES*

nce upon a time there was a poor man who had nothing at all, neither hearth nor home. What was he to do? He went into the forest, wove himself a wattle hut and settled down to live there.

He made his living by gathering firewood, taking it to town and selling it to buy some bread.

One day he set off for town with a bundle of firewood.

He sold it, bought some bread which he stuffed into his jerkin. Then off he trudged, cold and shivering, back to his wretched hut.

On the way he went past the king's palace.

The king's daughter saw him and said to her father:

*English translation © Raduga Publishers 1986

"Look, Father! The devil's coming!"

Her father looked out and saw it was a poor man, not the devil. He was angry with his daughter.

"That's not the devil. It's a man!"

"How can it be a man, all black and tattered!" said his daughter. "It's the devil, I tell you!"

The king and his daughter began to argue. The king was so enraged that he cried:

"Marry him at once or I'll have your head chopped off!"

His daughter was so afraid she decided to marry the poor man rather than lose her life.

So she tied some possessions in a bundle and ran after him, shouting:

"Wait there!"

The poor man turned round, but thinking that such a beautiful maid could not possibly be calling to him, he went on his way without looking back.

The poor man went into his hut and the princess followed him.

"Why have you come here?" the poor man asked.

"Because you must marry me," she said.

The poor man took fright. Why should he have such a wife? How could he feed her?

"You see how I make my living—by selling firewood to buy a crust of bread. How would I be able to keep you?" he said.

"Don't worry," she said. "I will keep myself and you too." Then she said:

"See this scarf that I have made. It costs five hundred gold pieces. The price is woven on it. Take it to the market and if anyone asks how much it costs say the price is woven on it. Sell it and bring home the money."

The poor man took the scarf and went off to market.

A merchant asked how much the scarf cost.

"The price is woven on it," said the poor man.

The merchant liked the scarf.

"Come home with me and I will pay you there," he said.

He took the poor man home, paid him the five hundred gold pieces, fed him and let him go.

The poor man brought the money home.

His wife wove another scarf with the same price on it, and gave it to her husband, saying:

"Take this to market too."

So he went to market with it. Try as he did, he just could not sell it.

Then a man asked the price and said:

"I have no money, but if you like I will give you three words of advice for it instead."

"No," said the poor man. "I will not sell it for words." Then he took the scarf and went off home.

"Didn't anyone want to buy it?" asked the wife.

"No," said the husband. "Someone offered me three words of advice for it, but I refused."

The wife got angry.

"Go back at once, find the man and give him the scarf in return for the three words of advice."

So off he went to market again. He looked and looked for the man, found him at last and said:

"I will give you the scarf for the three words of advice."

"Come with me," said the man.

He took him home and said:

"The first is this: say nothing without thinking first, but think and then say it. The second is this: if you are told

11

something about a person, no matter what it is, even that he wants to kill you, do not make haste to kill that person, but find out first whether it is true. And the third is this: if you are by a river and someone asks you if there is a ford there, it is not right to say carelessly that you think there is, for that person may go and get drowned. You should say that you don't know and the person must look for himself. Those are my three words of advice to you."

Then he gave the poor man rich presents and sent him home.

The poor man came home and told his wife the three words of advice.

"Be sure to remember them well," said his wife. "They will come in handy. Now it would be a good thing for you to find some work. Earn some money, bring it home and we will buy a team of oxen and live in plenty."

So off went the poor man to town. On the way he met three merchants.

"Good day, my man," said the merchants.

"Good day, my lords," the poor man replied.

"Will you come and work for us?"

"Why not? I will indeed."

"And how much shall we pay you a year?"

"Sixty pieces of gold."

The merchants gave him his wages for a year in advance.

The poor man took the money and sent it home with a fellow countryman, then followed the merchants.

They walked for three days and three nights without finding water.

Then they came to a mountain path and behind the mountain in a ravine was a spring.

The merchants gave the man a jug, saying:

"Bring us water from the ravine."

They were sending him to his death. That jug of water would cost him his life.

He came to the water and saw a handsome knight, all dressed in armour, playing with a frog.

The knight saw the poor man and said:

"Tell me, brother, who is more comely—me or this frog?"

The frog hopped about playfully on his shoulder.

The poor man was just about to say the first thing that came into his head, when he remembered the first word of advice, not to say anything without thinking first. He stepped back three paces, thought for a while and took fright. Suppose he said the knight was more comely than the frog then the knight got angry and killed him! There must be something behind it.

"Tell me. Why are you silent?" the knight kept urging him.

The poor man thought he'd better say that the frog was more comely.

"The frog is more comely!" he said.

This was just what the knight wanted. As soon as the poor man said the frog was more comely, the frog's skin burst open and out stepped a maid as fair as fair could be.

The handsome knight was beside himself with joy. He kissed the poor man and embraced him.

"How many have I slain by this spring to get that answer and deliver the enchanted princess from the magic spell! Now go and tell every man that the spring is free, for I am leaving here."

Before he went the knight gave the poor man three magic pomegranates and a woman's gold belt, saying:

"Take these pomegranates. They will be of use to you. And if you have a wife, let her wear this belt and she will bear you a son with golden curls."

Then he bade the poor man farewell and went off with his fair princess.

The poor man wrapped the pomegranates and gold belt in a cloth and sent them to his wife with a fellow country-man. Then he filled the jug and took it to the merchants. The merchants marvelled that he had come back alive and asked:

"Was there anyone by the spring?"

"There was, but he has gone," the poor man said. "The spring is free now."

Then they embraced the poor man and asked in amaze-ment:

"What did you say to make him leave the spring? We have suffered without water for so many years."

The fellow countryman gave the poor man's wife all the things wrapped up in the cloth.

The wife broke a pomegranate, and out of one half rose a splendid city with palaces and gardens.

She put horses, sheep and oxen to graze in the fields and

waited for her husband to return.

The poor man worked his twelve months. The merchants gave him more money for serving them well and sent him on his way.

They no longer needed a servant, for the spring was free. It was because of the spring that they had hired workmen.

The poor man set off home to his wattle hut.

On the way he saw some oxen grazing.

"Whose oxen are these?" he asked the herdsmen.

The herdsmen told him his own name.

He was vexed, even angered, thinking they were ridiculing him, but he said nothing and went on his way.

Then he saw some flocks of fine sheep and asked whose they were. Again he heard his own name.

He came to the forest and saw that his wattle hut had gone and in its place was a fine palace.

The poor man hesitated, then went into the courtyard.

"Where does such-and-such a woman live?" he asked about his wife.

"Our mistress? Up there in the palace on the hill," he was told.

The poor man marvelled, but could not make head or tail of it.

Servants appeared on all sides enquiring what he wanted. Was he looking for work perchance? Would he hire out his labour?

"Yes, I will," he said.

They all started talking noisily.

"We don't need him," some said.

"Yes, we do," said others.

Then an old goose-keeper said:

"I'll take him to look after the geese."

So they hired him.

A month passed. The poor man did his job looking after the geese.

One day he said to the old man:

"I want to see our mistress."

"I wouldn't make so bold as to go to her," said the old man. "But what if we sent the maid?"

They sent the maid, saying:

"Tell the mistress a man who has been working here for a month wants to see her."

The maid went and told the mistress.

The mistress came out onto the balcony, thinking it might be her husband, and ordered the servants to bring him to her.

He went with them wondering what would happen.

She saw him down below, recognised him and told the servants:

"Pick him up and carry him here so that his feet don't touch the ground."

The servants hastened to pick him up and shouted words of welcome, but tweaked him on the sly, angered that such honours should be shown to a simple goose-keeper.

They brought him to their mistress.

She sent all the servants away and attired him in fine raiment.

Then she took him by the arm and promenaded with him.

The servants were afraid when they heard that it was their master, thinking he would give them short shrift. But he was not angry and did not sack anyone. He just walked round the chambers surveying them.

In one chamber he saw a cradle with a gold-haired boy. He flew into a rage, seized his dagger and was about to run

and kill his wife, when he remembered the advice he had been given—think before you decide to kill someone. So he thought and remembered that he had sent her the gold belt and what the knight had said.

His wife came to him and said:

"All this you have earned by your labours. Remember how you sent me three pomegranates and a belt of gold. This city and palace all came out of one half of a magic pomegranate. And there are still two-and-a-half pomegranates left."

The man was overjoyed. They were as happy as the day is long.

Then one day the wife said:

"Invite my father to come and see us."

"Very well," the husband replied.

They chose a white horse from the herd, decked it with a silver saddle and silver harness, attired a servant in a fine white Circassian coat and sent him to invite the king.

"Do not tell anyone on the way," they enjoined him. "And do not tell the king himself that you are our servant. Say only that his son-in-law bade you invite him."

The servant went to the king and said:

"Your son-in-law bids you come and be his guest."

But the king only laughed and said to the servant:

"Are you not ashamed, fine fellow, to bear messages from that wretched beggar? Where did he get the courage to invite me, the king, to be his guest?"

The servant rode back and told them how the king had received him.

The next day they took a red horse from the herd, put a saddle of gold upon it, attired a servant in a golden robe and sent him to the king.

The servant arrived and said to the king:

"Gracious sire! Your son-in-law bids you do him the pleasure of being his guest."

Then the queen said to the king:

"Let us take servants and food, then call him out and give him some money. After all he is our son-in-law."

The servant rode off and announced that the king was coming and bringing his own food.

The king rode along and saw some flocks of sheep.

"Whose sheep are those?" he asked.

They named his son-in-law.

He rode further and saw some herds of horses grazing.

"Whose horses are those?" he asked.

Again they named his son-in-law.

The king looked at the horses, then told the servants to get rid of all the food and sent them all back.

"My son-in-law must have grown rich. It is shameful to go to him with my own food and servants."

He arrived and saw the splendid city and the palace where his daughter and her husband were promenading on the balcony.

The king and queen went up, embraced their daughter and son-in-law and kissed them.

"Why didn't you visit us before? Weren't we good enough for you?" asked the daughter.

They went into the banqueting hall.

The table was decked with all manner of refreshment such as the king had never seen before.

After they had dined the daughter said to her father: "I have something to sell you."

She brought out the two-and-a-half pomegranates, saying: "Buy these if you can."

The king paid her for the two pomegranates, but did not have enough money left to buy the half.

Then the king gave his son-in-law his blessing, hung his chain around his neck and set him on his throne.

THE FAIR MAID FROM FARAWAY NIGOZETI*

There was once a king who had three sons.

The father grew old, lost his sight and thought:

"I must find out which of my sons is most worthy to rule."

The old man summoned his eldest son and asked:

"Tell me what are the fullest, the fastest and the fairest things in the world. I want to see if you are worthy to rule. If your answers are right I will give you my throne."

Now the king had a magic horse. So this is what the eldest son replied:

"There is nothing in the world fuller than your horse, fairer than your wife (meaning his mother) and faster than your hounds."

*English translation © Raduga Publishers 1986

"No, my son. You are not worthy to rule," said the father and summoned his second son.

The second son said:

"The fairest thing is my wife, the fullest is my horse and the fastest is my hound."

"No, you are not worthy of my kingdom either," the father said and summoned his youngest son.

"You are my only hope now, my son—you must restore my sight and answer my riddles. Tell me what are the fullest, the fairest and the fastest things in the world."

The youngest son said:

"What can be fairer than spring, fuller and richer than autumn with its plentiful harvests and faster than our eye that reaches and encompasses all in an instant."

"Truly you alone are worthy of my kingdom," said the father. "And you will restore my sight too."

"Very well," said the son. "Only give me time to think."

Now the king had a horse. The young prince went to the horse, and the horse said to him:

"Why so pensive? Ask your father to give you a saddle with nine girths and his best sword and lash. When you mount me, strike me with the lash so hard that it strips the skin off me, and I will fly like the wind, so fast that no one will know if I have soared into the sky or plunged into

the bowels of the earth. When I stop, dismount and dig on that very spot and you will find the remedy for your father. Only seize it straightaway, or it will fly up into the heavens."

The youth did just as it said.

They galloped to the spot, he dismounted and dug in the ground. All of a sudden something like snow flew out of the ground and up into the sky. Then it melted so quickly that he did not have time to even see it, let alone take hold of it.

The horse said:

"It won't come down for a whole week, so rather than wait here, let us be on our way. Today the King of the East is marching to wage war on the King of the West. He wishes to enslave him. We must intervene and help the hard-pressed sovereign."

The youth looked and saw something moving along, all black with dust. It was the King of the East's army.

So the youth sped along on his horse and plunged into the fray.

The horse trampled them down with its hooves, while the youth hacked right and left with his sword, until he slayed them all but the king who managed to flee with his counsellors.

The King of the West looked through his spy-glass and saw his enemies dead and fleeing.

"Who has done me this great service of destroying my foes?" he exclaimed in amazement.

The youth's little finger had been cut in the fray and he sent a message to the king.

"Pray send me something to bind my hand."

Send indeed! They all hastened to him, clustered about him and led him to the palace with due honours. Then they took him to his chamber and laid him down to rest. And they led his horse to the stables, took off the saddle, rubbed it down, covered it with a horse-cloth and fed it with raisins and almonds.

The courtiers envied the youth and feared he would become the king's favourite.

So they went and told the king:

"This youth can find enough ivory to build a whole palace. Tell him to do so."

When the youth came to breakfast, the king said to him:

"Build me a palace of ivory."

"Give me time to think," said the youth.

When he went and told the horse.

"That's not hard to do," the horse said. "Only ask the

king for a hundred wineskins, each one with a hundred gallons, and a big pile of fleece, and we'll build him a palace of ivory."

The youth did as he was told.

They gave him the wine and the fleece, and he set off for the land where elephants dwell.

He came there and saw a mountain with nine ice-cold springs. The springs all flowed together. This was where the elephants came to drink.

The youth blocked the water with some fleece and made it flow in the opposite direction. With the rest of the fleece and some rocks he made a pool and poured the wine into it.

"Now look and see if the elephants are lying down or coming to drink," said the horse.

"I can see a group of them," the youth replied.

"Then they will soon be here," said the horse.

They hid.

The elephants came to the watering place, but there was no water.

They tried the wine, but did not like the taste and moved away. But they were tormented by thirst. What were they to do?

They stood awhile and looked around, until thirst drove

them back and they began to drink the wine. They grew tipsy and collapsed onto the ground.

"Now get your sword and cut off their tusks," the horse ordered.

They took as many as they could and piled up the rest to collect next time.

They arrived laden with the ivory.

The courtiers could not believe their eyes.

"He's come back safe and sound!"

And the youth built an ivory palace with nails of gold.

The king was delighted, but the courtiers came to him and said:

"What a splendid fellow you have found. But that's nothing! He can catch the Fire-Bird, put it in a cage and hang it on the palace wall, so the whole world will marvel at its singing."

The king summoned the youth and said:

"Bring me the Fire-Bird."

"Give me until tomorrow to think about it," said the youth.

He went to the horse.

"The king wants me to get him the Fire-Bird."

"Don't worry," said the horse. "Ask him for nine wineskins

of millet, ten hundred weight each, and we will bring him the Fire-Bird too."

The king gave them the millet, and they set off for distant lands.

At last they came to some mountains with flocks of birds twittering and trilling all manner of songs.

"Now lay down and cover yourself with millet," said the horse. "The birds will fly down, and the Fire-Bird will sit on top, right over your heart. It will peck you one, two, three times, and then you must grab it rightaway or you will never catch it."

The youth lay down and covered himself with millet.

Down flew the Fire-Bird followed by all the other birds, twittering and trilling all manner of songs.

They settled and began to peck.

The Fire-Bird pecked once, then twice, but as soon as it pecked the third time, the youth grabbed it and jumped up. The other birds flew at him, pecking, scratching and beating him with their wings until the poor youth could bear it no longer. Then up galloped the horse, drove the birds away and sped off with the youth and the Fire-Bird.

When the youth arrived back, the courtiers could hardly believe their eyes. Here he was again safe and sound

with the Fire-Bird!

They went and told the king:

"Tell him, if he is such a clever fellow, to bring you the fair maid from faraway Nigozeti to be your bride."

The king summoned the youth and said:

"Bring me the fair maid from faraway Nigozeti to be my bride."

The youth went and told the horse.

The horse thought for a while.

"That is no easy task! The trouble is this. The fair maid in the land of Nigozeti has a mare who is my sister. She is stronger and faster than I. I fear she will get the better of us. But there's nothing for it. We must go. Only remember that the fair maid lives in a castle. The east door is unbolted, but the west door is closed. And by the doors a goat and a wolf are chained. The goat has a bone and the wolf a bundle of hay. And it is there that my sister, the mare, stands guard too. Bolt the east door and open the west, give the hay to the goat and the bone to the wolf, and I will see to my sister the mare. The fair maid sits in the castle with her long, long hair flowing down. Go in and wind the hair as fast as you can onto your arm. If you are fast enough she will be yours, if not she will be the death of us."

They came to the castle. The youth threw the goat's bone to the wolf and gave the hay to the goat, then he opened the west door, sped into the castle, bolted the east door, ran up to the fair maid and wound her hair round his arm in a flash.

"Save me, east doors!" cried the fair maid.

"At long last someone has bolted us and given our hinges a rest. Why should we open again?" said the east doors.

"Save me, west doors!"

"At long last someone has opened us and given our hinges an airing. Why should we close again?" said the west doors.

"Save me, goat!"

"At long last I've got some hay. Why should I leave it?"

"Save me, wolf!"

"It's the first time anyone's given me a bone," said the wolf. "I won't leave it."

The fair maid called to the mare.

"Save me, my trusty servant!"

"How can I? I can't even get the better of my brother," said the mare.

So the youth won the fair maid from the land of Nigozeti

47

and took her to the king.

When they arrived, the fair maid said:

"I shall not come before the king until they have set up a big bath of marble and filled it with boiling milk to bathe in."

They set up the bath and filled it with boiling milk.

"Tell His Majesty I will receive him," said the fair maid.

The king arrived.

"Kindly be the first to bathe," said the maid.

The king went up to look at the bath, and the maid gave him such a hefty push that he fell into the milk and boiled to death.

Then they threw all the courtiers in as well, until no one was left.

So the youth got the East kingdom and the West kingdom and the fair maid from faraway Nigozeti.

Then it was time for the remedy for blindness to fall down from the sky and sink into the ground again. The youth galloped off on his horse and just managed to catch it before it touched the ground.

So the youth rode off home with the fair maid and the remedy for blindness. His blind father was overjoyed that his son had returned triumphant.

"I have brought you this remedy for blindness, father, and have won this fair maid from faraway Nigozeti to be my bride, and two kingdoms to boot," the son told his father the glad tidings.

His father's sight returned, they had a splendid wedding and then lived happily ever after.

ARMENIAN FOLK TALE

Azaran Bulbul

Retold by *Yakov Khachatriants*

Translated by *Avril Pyman*

Illustrations by *Felix Giulanian*

AZARAN BULBUL

Once upon a time there lived a king. He had three sons: two clever, and the third—a simpleton. The simpleton was called Alo Dino. And the king also had a beautiful garden and in the garden an apple-tree on which grew only three apples.

One day a beggar came to the garden and asked the gardener: "Give me one of those three apples."

"No-o," said the gardener. "They are not to be touched. Only the king may pick them!"

The beggar grew angry and put a curse on the garden. Immediately the whole garden withered.

"What have you done?" exclaimed the gardener in horror. "Will our garden never bloom again?"

"It will not bloom," said the old man, "until you have caught the bird called Azaran Bulbul."

Then the king came, saw that the garden had withered and began to reproach the gardener.

The gardener told him about the wandering beggar.

"What are we to do now?" cried the king. "Who will go and capture Azaran Bulbul?"

The eldest son heard the king and said:

"Father, I will go and capture Azaran Bulbul!"

And after him the middle son spoke.

"Father, I will go and capture Azaran Bulbul."

"Go, both of you, and bring me this bird," was the doom spoken by their father.

Meanwhile the youngest son, Alo Dino, had been out for a walk. When he came back he saw that his brothers were gone. He asked his mother:

"Where are my brothers?"

"You are a foolish lad," said the mother. "You don't know anything. Your brothers have gone on a quest for the bird called Azaran Bulbul."

Alo Dino, without stopping to think, ran off to the head groom:

"Choose me a good horse, I am going on a journey."

"There are the horses. Take which you like," replied the groom.

Alo Dino began to choose a horse. But whenever he touched

one it would sink to the ground, so heavy was his hand. Alo Dino left the stables and saw at the gate a shaggy, dirty horse which nobody cared for. Alo Dino clapped him on the back and the horse kept his legs as though there was nothing to it. Alo Dino ordered the groom to bathe the horse three times a day and to feed him on raisins—a *pood** an hour.

Three days later Alo Dino mounted his horse and set off. Soon he caught up with his brothers.

At the sight of Alo Dino the eldest brother was annoyed.

"Why did you have to come trailing after us? Want to put us to shame, do you?" he shouted, and struck Alo Dino.

But here the middle brother intervened:

"That's enough, don't strike him. Let him come with us. He can be our attendant."

The three of them continued on their way together. They rode for a long time until they came to a crossroads, where the road branched off in three directions. At the crossroad sat an old man.

"Good health to you, Grandfather!" the brothers greeted him.

*_Pood_— 36 lbs avoirdupois.

"Good health to you, Princes!"

"Whither do these roads lead?" asked the eldest.

"One," replied the old man, "leads to Tbilisi, another—to Yerevan. And the third is an evil road of no return. That is its name: Gedan Gyalmaz (The wayfarer will not return)."

"You two take the safe roads," said the youngest brother. "I shall take the road Gedan Gyalmaz".

"Let him go, a good riddance to the simpleton," the eldest brother decided.

The eldest and the middle brother had to endure much hardship. To save themselves from starvation they sold their horses and their clothes and finally hired themselves out to work at a public baths, one as a stoker, the other as a bath attendant.

Alo Dino, on the other hand, rode on and on along the road Gedam Gyalmaz, until he came at last to the Red Land. Trees, stones and earth—all were red. And suddenly his horse spoke out in a human voice:

"Alo Dino, do you know where you and I have landed ourselves? This is the country of the three-headed Red Dev."

Towards evening Alo Dino arrived at the house of the Red Dev.

At the gates stood a woman. She saw Alo Dino and took pity on him.

"Let me hide you, laddy."

"Nonsense," replied Alo Dino. "I'd rather you gave me something to eat. I'm hungry."

The Dev's wife went and brought Alo Dino two or three platefuls of food.

"What's this you've brought! You've only whetted my appetite! I said, give me something to eat!"

"If that is not enough for you go on into the courtyard. The Dev's dinner is set out there—eat to your heart's content."

Alo Dino went into the courtyard where he saw 5 *lidrs** of rice and two roasted oxen. In three goes he ate all the pilaff and both oxen. Again the Dev's wife took pity on him:

"You're risking your life to no purpose, laddy, I'm sorry for you. Let me hide you."

"I'm not afraid of your Dev!" said Alo Dino. "It's him I came for."

Suddenly he noticed that the house was shaking.

"What's the house shaking for?"

*Lidr—about 18 pounds.

"Because the Dev is coming," replied the woman.

The Dev was getting nearer. He drove before him a whole pack of wolves, foxes and other wild animals. Having rounded them up in the courtyard he entered his house, saw Alo Dino and said:

"Welcome, Alo Dino!"

"How do you know who I am?" asked Alo Dino.

"The day you were born I was walking in the mountains and the rocks, trees and grasses all proclaimed your coming into the world. So I think that you must be Alo Dino for no one else would dare cross the threshold of my house."

Then the Dev turned to his wife:

"Well, wife, give us something to eat."

"That lad there ate up all your dinner," said his wife, "and didn't leave you anything."

The Dev said nothing but slit the throats of a couple of wolves, his wife prepared a meal and they all sat down to dine. The Dev noticed that Alo Dino did not throw away the bones but ate them together with the meat. After dinner the Dev said:

"Shall we fight now, Alo Dino, or shall we postpone it till the morning?"

"As you will, I'm always ready."

Next morning the Dev and Alo Dino woke at first light. Each took his club.

Alo Dino said:

"Your turn, you begin,—I'm the guest."

"On guard—my throw."

At this point Alo Dino's horse whispered to his master:

"When the Dev raises his arm you hit me with the whip, I will jump and the Dev's club will pass beneath me!"

And so they did. Three times the Dev threw his club— and each time he missed!

"Now it is my turn," said Alo Dino and, advancing on the Dev, knocked off all three heads with one sweep of his club. After which he cut off the lips and noses, put them in his pack and went to pay his respects to the Dev's widow.

"Good health, sister-in-law!" he said.

"I am not your sister-in-law. I want to be your wife."

"I cannot marry you," said Alo Dino. "You will be the wife of my eldest brother."

Three days later Alo Dino decided to move on.

"Where are you going now?" asked the Dev's widow.

"I am going to capture Azaran Bulbul!"

"I beg you, do not go: you will be risking your life to no purspose—it is a very difficult quest."

"No, it is my duty to go."

And so Alo Dino came to a land where the earth and the trees and the rocks were all white.

"Know, you!" said the horse. "This is the country of the White Dev. This evening we will be guests in his house. He is not like the Red Dev; he has seven heads."

"Never mind," replied Alo Dino. "I'll chop off all seven for him."

In the evening they came to the Dev's abode, but the doors of the Dev were locked. Alo Dino said in a loud voice:

"Hey, who's there?"

At his call a woman appeared, opened the door and showed Alo Dino where to stable his horse. Alo Dino led the horse away, then entered the Dev's rooms and asked his wife for something to eat. She brought him five or six great dishes of pilaff.

"What do you take me for, a child? I'm telling you I want something to eat."

The Dev's wife said:

"Go up to the Dev's table and eat as much as you wish."

Alo Dino saw a huge pot on the table in which there were twenty *lidrs* of pilaff and three roast oxen. In two goes Alo Dino polished off the pilaff and the oxen. Suddenly the house began to shake.

"Laddy, that's the Dev coming; let me hide you," said the Dev's wife.

"Don't worry," said Alo Dino. "It's your Dev I came for."

Soon the Dev himself appeared. He was driving a multitude of different animals before him—lions, wolves and bears. The Dev rounded them up in the courtyard, mounted the steps of his house, saw Alo Dino and stretched out his hand:

"Good health, Alo Dino!"

"How do you know that I am Alo Dino?"

"When you were born the mountains, the rocks, the trees and the grasses told me that you had come into the world. You are Alo Dino, because no one else would have dared to call in on me here."

He asked his wife for something to eat. She replied that the guest had finished off the entire dinner.

"All right," said the Dev. "We'll prepare a dinner from what I've just brought in."

Soon the dinner was served. The Dev noticed that his guest

ate the meat together with the bones.

"Shall we begin the fight now?" the Dev enquired after dinner.

"As you will—I'm ready!" replied Alo Dino.

"No, we'll leave it till the morning," the Dev decided. "It is our custom to give the guest good cheer in the evening and to fight him in the morning!"

Early next morning Alo Dino shouted:

"Get up, it's time for us to fight!"

The Dev got up, took his club and came out onto the *Maidan.**

When Alo Dino mounted his horse it whispered to him:

"Strike me with your whip, I will jump and the Dev's club will pass beneath me."

"Throw!" shouted the Dev.

"You first!" answered Alo Dino. "I am the guest."

"On guard—my throw."

Three times the Dev whirled the club and at last threw it. But Alo Dino's horse managed to leap up in time and the Dev's club flew beneath his stomach touching neither him

Maidan—square, tilt-yard.

66

nor his rider. In the dust which they raised the Dev could not see Alo Dino and decided that he must be dead. The Dev laughed.

"Come now, where are you, Alo Dino? I'll soon smell you out!"

"Here I am, brother, no need to trouble yourself, hold tight now!" answered Alo Dino, spurred his horse and fell upon the Dev.

With one stroke of his sable he cut off the Dev's seven heads. Then he dismounted, cut off the lips and noses of his slain opponent, stuffed them into his pack and returned to the Dev's house.

"Beloved," said the Dev's wife. "What a good thing that you have slain the Dev! Take me to be your wife!"

"No, you will be the wife of my middle brother," said Alo Dino. And began to prepare for the next stage of his journey.

"Where are you going, dear heart?" asked the Dev's wife.

"After Azaran Bulbul."

"But you will never get him!" said she.

"I *must* get him," said Alo Dino, and set forth.

When he came to the land of the Black Dev, his horse

again began to speak:

"Alo Dino, this is the country of the forty-headed Black Dev. Look, here the earth and the stones and the trees and the grasses are all black."

Alo Dino entered the Dev's house and saw there a vast cauldron with forty *lidrs* of rice pilaff, and across the rice lay four roast oxen. Alo Dino knocked back all the pilaff in four goes, then swallowed the oxen, wiped his mouth and went on into the Black Dev's private apartments.

Towards evening the house began to shake. It was the Dev coming in with his trophies from the hunt. On seeing Alo Dino, the Dev came up to him and said:

"Hail, Alo Dino!"

"How do you know who I am?"

"The stones, the mountains, the trees and the grasses all announced the news of your birth," replied the Dev and then, turning to his wife, asked for something to eat.

"Alo Dino has eaten you dinner," she answered.

"Never mind, cook something up from what I've brought in."

After dinner they lay down to sleep. They rose with the dawn and began to fight. For three days and three nights they fought, but neither could get the better of the other. At last Alo Dino succeeded in slaying the Dev, cut off his lips and his noses, stuffed them into his pack and returned to the Dev's private apartments. The Dev's wife was overjoyed.

"Take me as your wife," she said.

"All right," said Alo Dino and became sunk in thought.

"What are you thinking about?"

"Our garden has withered," answered Alo Dino, "I went to fetch Azaran Bulbul, and now I got stuck here."

"It's no easy matter to capture Azaran Bulbul," said the Dev's widow. "His master is King Chachonts. He has been asleep for the last forty days. But when he wakes up he will be fit to kill even forty such heroes as you."

"Well, I shall go anyway," said Alo Dino. "And when I come back I shall marry you."

He took leave of her and set forth on his way.

When he came to the sea his horse said:

"I am no sea horse, I cannot cross the sea."

Alo Dino dismounted, laid his head on a stone and went to sleep. Suddenly he heard a voice in his sleep:

"Alo Dino! Under the stone which is serving you as a pillow there are three sea-horse reins buried. Gird yourself

with two of the reins and make a cast with the third into the sea." Alo Dino rose, raised the stone and found three reins, just as the voice had promised. Two reins he girded about himself and the end of the third rein he threw into the sea. Immediately a sea horse appeared and tried to swallow Alo Dino, but Alo Dino kept his presence of mind, seized the horse by the mane and leapt on its back. Then the horse spoke in human tongue:

"Tell me, Alo Dino, what it is you want, and I will do your will."

"I want Azaran Bulbul."

"I cannot get him for you, but I will carry you across the sea to where my elder sister lives and she will help you to find Azaran Bulbul."

And the horse bore Alo Dino across to the other side. But here Alo Dino forgot to take off the rein and the horse galloped off with it back into the sea.

"Oh, what shall I do now? The horse has carried off the third rein!" exlaimed Alo Dino.

For a long time he wandered about the island, lost in thought.

Then his hand chanced to wander to his belt and he remembered that he had girded himself with two reins and was very glad.

Alo Dino took off one of the reins and threw the end into the sea. A sea mare immediately came plunging up out of the water and tried to swallow Alo Dino, but he at once leapt astride her.

"Tell me what you want, I'll do anything," said the mare.

"I want Azaran Bulbul!" replied Alo Dino.

"That is a very difficult matter," replied the mare. "Azaran Bulbul's cage hangs in the palace of King Chachonts and the palace stands on the very edge of the sea. If you can strike me a blow with your whip to set all the three hundred and sixty veins in my body a-tremble, then I will fly up to the window of the palace and you will stretch out your hand and seize the cage. But if you do not catch it in time then know that we shall both fall and perish."

"All right," said Alo Dino and gave the mare a blow with his knout which set her liver aflame and all the three hundred and sixty veins in her body a-tremble.

She went soaring up into the air and flew to the window. Alo Dino stretched out his hand and seized the cage. As they returned to earth the mare said:

"Now let me go."

Alo Dino let her go and set off on the return journey. He found his own horse and, together with the bird Azaran Bulbul, they returned to the country of the Black Dev. He greeted his wife and turned to the bird.

"Dear Bulbul, speak, and all these black mountains will become green."

Azaran Bulbul spoke and the black mountains were covered with rich verdure. Alo Dino's wife was amazed at the power of Azaran Bulbul.

They collected all the treasures of the Black Dev and went to the land of the White Dev. Here also they seized the treasures of the Dev, took the second brother's promised wife, mounted their horses and rode on to the land of the Red Dev. And here also they seized the goods of the Dev, took his wife and so came at last to the old man who was still sitting at the same spot where the road forked off in three directions.

"Hail, Grandfather," said Alo Dino. "How goes it with my brothers? Have they returned?"

"No, Prince, no one has returned," answered the old man.

"If that is so," said Alo Dino, "I will leave these three

women and the bird in your care and I will go for my brothers."

Alo Dino sought his brothers through many cities and could not find them. In one town he was invited to the home of one of the citizens. He asked his host:

"How can I find out what foreigners are living in your town?"

"Go to the bazaar in the morning," replied his host, "and let it be known that you want to organise a feast for vagrants and wanderers. As soon as the vagrants hear about it they will all come running and it will be easy for you to find the ones you are looking for."

Early in the morning Alo Dino bought seven oxen and ordered them to be slain and roasted, then he rang the bell in the bell-tower.

Hearing the peal of bells, Alo Dino's two brothers, the bath attendant and the stoker, asked their master what was going on.

"They are summoning all the foreigners to a feast," their master answered.

The brothers begged to be released from their duties to attend the feast. All the vagrants in the town were met together.

Seeing his brothers, Alo Dino brought them wine and meat and asked:

"Do you recognise me?"

"No," they answered.

"Where do you work?"

"In the public baths, one of us is a stoker, the other—an attendant."

Alo Dino took his brothers to the owner of the baths and said:

"Settle your accounts with them. They go with me."

"And what relation are they to you?"

"They are my brothers."

Then the eldest brother said:

"We do not know you. Who are you?"

"I'm Alo Dino. Eh, you block-heads!"

"If you are our brother," said the eldest, "tell us what we left home to find?"

"Azaran Bulbul. I have brought him."

"Where is he?"

"With that old man at the crossroads—let us go, I will show you."

Alo Dino bought his brothers new clothes, they dressed

up and all three went back to the old man.

Seeing the three women with the old man the brothers asked:

"Who are those women?"

"That one," said Alo Dino, "is the wife of the Red Dev whom I slew." Here he got the lips of the Red Dev and showed them to his brother. "Now she will be your wife, Eldest. And that one is the wife of the White Dev, whom I also slew, see his noses and his lips—she will be the wife of our middle brother. And that third one, the wife of the Black Dev—is my wife."

The brothers took Azaran Bulbul, mounted their horses, each taking up his bride before him, and all together set out on the homeward journey.

The way was long and at last they came upon a well in a wood.

"Alo Dino," said the brothers, "climb down the well, we are thirsty."

When she heard this, Alo Dino's wife went up close to her husband:

"Alo Dino," she whispered, "don't go down: they are planning to kill you."

"No," answered Alo Dino. "My brothers want to drink, and I will go down the well!"

"Then take my glove and slipper," she said, "and keep them well. Later I shall claim them from the king and if they are found and brought to the palace I shall know that you have managed to get out of the well."

Alo Dino climbed down into the well and the brothers, seizing Azaran Bulbul and the women, continued on their way. As they came to the town, the brothers sent a messenger to the king.

The king assembled all the people and came out to meet his sons and to convey them home with great honour. Then the king asked:

"Who are these women with you?"

"That one," said the elder brother, "is my wife, that one is the middle son's wife, and that one is to be our servant."

"Sire, what he says is not true," said Alo Dino's wife. "I am no wife of his."

"I see, my children, that you are at odds between yourselves and I cannot make out which of you it was who captured Azaran Bulbul. Whoever can induce Azaran Bulbul to speak is no doubt the one."

"Let me, I shall make him speak," said the eldest, and addressed Azaran Bulbul: "Sweet Bulbul, speak, that our garden may come into leaf again."

Azaran Bulbul answered not a word.

Then the middle son stepped forth.

"Bulbul, dear," said he, "speak, that our garden may come into bloom again."

Azaran Bulbul was silent.

The people wondered, and the garden lay waste as before. So now let us return to Alo Dino.

How long he sat there at the bottom of the well no one knows. At last a merchant came to the well and ordered his servants to draw water. Alo Dino, hearing voices, shouted:

"Help me out! I'll bring you all the water you need."

They let down the bucket into the well and filled it with water, as much as they needed, then they let down a rope and ten to fifteen men hauled Alo Dino out of the well.

The merchant asked how Alo Dino came to be at the bottom of the well. Alo Dino replied:

"I am a wandering traveller. I was walking at night, it was dark. I did not notice the well and fell in."

"Where are you going?"

"To my own town," answered Alo Dino.

That night Alo Dino spent with the merchant. They had supper together and lay down to sleep. In the morning they resumed their separate ways. When Alo Dino came to his father's town he settled down to live with a certain old man to whom he became as a son.

Once the old man saw the king's men walking about the town showing a glove to all the passers-by and crying:

"The king gives his son in marriage! Who can sew another glove like this one for the bride?"

The old man told this to Alo Dino. Then Alo Dino left him and offered himself as apprentice to a tailor. The tailor did not know that he was of the blood royal and accepted him. Alo Dino was an obedient apprentice—he cleaned out the shop and did everything that was required of him.

Meanwhile the viziers and the nazirs of the king went from one tailor to the next showing the glove. They called also at the shop where Alo Dino was working and asked the tailor if he would not sew another such glove. The master-craftsman refused. Suddenly the new apprentice stepped out and advised the tailor to accept the order.

"I can sew the glove!" he said.

"You're out of your mind!" said the tailor. "You only began your apprenticeship yesterday and today you're already offering to take on a job like that."

"Let him try," the king's men interceded. "But," they added, "if he can't, the king will cut off his head."

"All right," agreed Alo Dino.

The tailor couldn't believe his ears:

"You are throwing your life away for no good reason! I have been working at the tailor's trade these twenty years and that workmanship is beyond me, but you..."

"Never fear, Master! If you buy me five *poods* of small nuts, I will manage it."

The tailor went out and bought four *poods*.

"Why did you buy a *pood* too little?"

"Not enough money," replied the tailor.

Alo Dino ate nuts all night long. The next morning the tailor came to his shop and saw: beside the Royal glove lay another, exactly the same. The tailor wanted to take it in his hands for a better look, but Alo Dino said:

"Don't touch it, Master, you'll spoil it!"

Soon the nazir and the vizier appeared on the scene.

"Well, how goes it, Master? Is our order ready?"

The tailor was dumb with terror and did not answer. Alo Dino came forward and showed the glove. The nazir and the vizier were astonished.

"Well, Master, let us go to the king," said the nazir and the vizier. "He will pay you for your work."

"Go with them to the king, Master, and receive the reward for the work," said Alo Dino.

"No-no, son, I shall not go. You go. What if the work just doesn't happen to take his fancy? Let him cut off your head, not mine."

Alo Dino went to the palace. When the glove was shown to the king, he said:

"I have no understanding of such things. Show it to my daughter-in-law."

The daughter-in-law was pleased with the work and she gave three hundred rubles for the master-craftsman. To which the king added two hundred from his own coffers.

Alo Dino returned to the shop and spread out the money before the tailor:

"There, Master, it's all yours!"

The tailor was delighted and took the money. Then Alo Dino said:

"You're a bad man, Master."

"Why?"

"Because I asked you for five *poods* of nuts and you bought only four. I shall not stay with you any longer!" And Alo Dino went to a cobbler's workshop.

"Master," Alo Dino said to the cobbler. "I am an orphan, I have no one to care for me. Take pity on me, teach me your trade."

The cobbler took him into his house.

A day or two later the nazir and the vizier came to the cobbler. They showed a slipper and asked the cobbler if he would not stitch another like it. He was on the point of refusing when Alo Dino came forward and said that he would stitch such a slipper.

"You've only just entered my business and you are prepared to take on work like that?" said the cobbler angrily.

"Don't be angry, Master, I'll manage it," Alo Dino soothed him.

"But," said the vizier, "if you do not, the king will have both your heads."

"Don't take it on," said the cobbler. "Pity me, an old man!"

"Don't be afraid, Master, I'll manage it. If you buy me twenty *poods* of nuts, I'll stitch you that slipper in one night."

The master bought him nineteen *poods* of nuts.

"Now, Master, you go off home, and I'll work," Alo Dino said to the cobbler.

The cobbler, very worried, went home. But he could not wait till morning: in the middle of the night he came back and began to watch Alo Dino from a place of concealment. Seeing that Alo Dino was eating nuts, the cobbler began to curse under his breath: "What the devil possessed me to take up with such an idler! I'll lose my head and all for nothing!"

As dawn was breaking the cobbler entered his shop and suddenly saw, side by side with the first slipper, another exactly like it. He stretched out a hand to take the slipper, but Alo Dino said:

"Yesterday you did not want to take on the work, so today I shall not allow you to touch the slipper!"

Soon the nazir and the vizier came and were very pleased with the cobbler's work.

"Now," said they, "one of you will come with us to the king to receive the reward for your work."

"You had better go, my son," the cobbler said to Alo Dino. "After all, the king may not fancy the slipper."

Alo Dino went to the palace. The slippers were taken to the king, who immediately ordered them to be shown to his daughter-in-law.

The daughter-in-law guessed at once that these were her own slippers, and recognised Alo Dino.

"Why do you tarry?" she asked.

"My time is not yet!" replied Alo Dino.

The daughter-in-law of the king gave the craftsmen five hundred rubles. And the king added another five hundred from his own coffers.

Alo Dino took the money back to the cobbler.

"Here, Master, is the money. But I shall leave you."

"Why?"

"I asked you for twenty *poods* of nuts and you only bought me nineteen."

And Alo Dino returned to the old man.

"Where have you been, sonny?" the old man asked.

"I'm a young lad, I've been on the town," replied Alo Dino and gave the old man ten handfuls of gold.

Some time later the old man saw a great number of troops

arrayed in the market place and heard that this was King Chachonts who had come with his army and was looking for whoever it was who had stolen Azaran Bulbul from his palace. When he heard this, Alo Dino said to the old man:

"Go, Father, to our king and say: 'Lend your own horse to my son; he will go and parley with King Chachonts riding that horse.'"

The old man went to the court. The king said:

"Ever since they brought back the horse he has been standing in his stall: no one dares approach him."

The king's daughter-in-law guessed that it was her husband who had sent the old man to the king and begged the king's permission to lead out the horse herself.

The king granted her request and his daughter-in-law led the horse out of his stall and gave him to the old man. The old man took him to Alo Dino.

Alo Dino rode his horse out onto the town square. There he met his elder brother.

"Where are you going?" asked Alo Dino.

"It was I who took the bird Bulbul, and now I go to King Chachonts to answer for my deed," replied his brother and turned his horse towards the army of King Chachonts.

"Where is the king's tent?"

"Over there, the red one!"

The eldest son entered the red tent of the king and bowed before him seven times.

"Are you the prince?" asked King Chachonts.

"As it please you."

"You kidnapped Azaran Bulbul?"

"As it please you."

"How did you get him?"

"I took him down from a tree in your forest."

"A poor story, brother: it was not you who took the Bulbul," said the king.

The prince returned home. Then the middle brother mounted his horse and went to King Chachonts.

"Where are you going?" asked Alo Dino.

"It was I who took the bird Bulbul, and now I go to King Chachonts to answer for my deed."

He entered the tent of the king and bowed seven times.

"So it is you who kidnapped Azaran Bulbul?" asked King Chachonts.

"As it please you."

"Come then, tell me what happened?"

"It was dark. I saw the bird suddenly come flying down to settle on its nest. I stretched out a hand and—snap—there I was holding the Bulbul."

"A poor story, it was not you who captured the Bulbul."

After that King Chachonts issued a royal ultimatum. "Find me the man who took Azaran Bulbul or I will lay waste the whole country."

Alo Dino came before the king his father and asked his permission to go and to answer to the ultimatum. The king did not recognise his son and said:

"All right, go if you want."

"King," Alo Dino said. "Let us make a bargain. If King Chachonts goes away, you will surrender your power to me for three hours."

The king agreed. Alo Dino rode over to King Chachonts.

"Are you a prince?" asked King Chachonts.

"As it please you."

"You kidnapped Azaran Bulbul?"

"As it please you, King. It was I who captured Azaran Bulbul."

"Tell me how it happened."

Alo Dino told everything just as it had occurred.

"So you're Alo Dino?" asked the king with astonishment.

"As it please you."

"But how am I to believe that it was you who performed all those great deeds?"

Alo Dino immediately took his pack and showed the King the lips and noses of the three Devs.

Then King Chachonts said:

"My son, I make you a present of my bird!" and, calling up his army, departed whence he had come.

On returning to his father, Alo Dino said:

"Do you not recognise me?"

"No."

"I am your son Alo Dino!"

"If you are in truth my son, make our garden come into leaf again."

Alo Dino went up to Azaran Bulbul and said:

"Bird, dear heart, speak, that our garden may bloom again."

The bird began to speak and the garden came into leaf at that very moment.

Then Alo Dino said to the king,

"You promised that for three hours the kingdom should be mine."

"Yes, that is your right," agreed the king.

Alo Dino sat upon the throne and called his brothers to judgement. The brothers confessed everything.

"How should they be punished, Sire?" Alo Dino asked his father.

"My son, that is as you will."

Alo Dino said:

"They did not kill me, so I will not kill them. Let them and their wives leave our country."

And the brothers went away.

AZERBAIJAN FOLK TALES

Ibrahim the Orphan and the Greedy Shopkeeper

Retold by *Akhliman Akhundov*

Translated by *K. M. Cook*

The Story of Zarniyar Who Had All Her Wits About Her

Retold by *Mikhail Bulatov*

Translated by *Irina Zheleznova*

Illustrations by *Togrul Narimanbekov*

IBRAHIM THE ORPHAN
AND THE GREEDY SHOPKEEPER*

Once upon a time there was a fowler and his wife. They lived a hard life: many a time hunger made them bemoan their wretched lot. From time to time the fowler would go off to foreign lands and catch birds there, which he then sold for a pittance, thereby eking out a miserable existence. His wife worked for some rich folk, but her wages were only enough to buy bread. Then fate dealt her an even harder blow: her husband, with whom she had shared both joy and sorrow, suddenly died.

The poor widow was left alone to look after not only herself but also her young son Ibrahim.

When Ibrahim reached the age of twelve, he could no longer bear to see his mother so emaciated from endless toil and cares.

One day he asked her:

*English translation © Raduga Publishers 1986

"Do I have a father, mother? If so, where is he and what is his trade?"

"You did have a father," his mother told him. "But he died. He was a fowler by trade and left you his net and pipe for catching birds."

"Where are they?" Ibrahim asked.

"In that chest over there," replied his mother, pointing to it.

Ibrahim ran over to the chest, got out the net and pipe and began to examine them. Then he resolved to take up his father's trade.

He told his mother that he was going fowling and asked her to prepare him food for the journey. His mother was surprised at her son's sudden decision and enquired where he planned to go. Ibrahim told her that he intended to see the world. This troubled the poor mother greatly, and she began to prepare her son for his travels with tears in her eyes. In return for a promise to work six months for him she borrowed a little money from a rich man. With this money the unfortunate mother bought her son some clothes and bread and cheese for the journey.

Early next morning Ibrahim bade his mother farewell and set off. He walked all day and all night and on the third day found himself at the edge of a forest. Here Ibrahim built

himself a hut to live in for a while. No sooner had he laid out his net and begun to play his pipe, than a strange bird appeared.

Each of its feathers was a different colour.

Ibrahim could not take his eyes off it, and great was his joy when the bird suddenly got trapped in his net. He seized it quickly with the net and, without further ado, sped home to tell his mother of his good fortune.

Ibrahim's mother was overjoyed that her son had come back with such a fine catch. She was sure that anyone would be glad to buy the bird. Ibrahim did not propose to sell it, however. He put the bird in a cage and began to admire its beauty.

After a while the bird laid an egg. Mother and son were delighted when they saw that the egg was as beautiful and many-coloured as the bird itself. Ibrahim's mother took the egg and went to the shopkeeper.

The shopkeeper gave her a little money for the egg and promised to pay twice as much if she brought him another one. The happy mother returned home happily. Then the shopkeeper made haste and went off to town to present the egg to the Shah. The Shah was overjoyed at the gift and rewarded him lavishly.

No sooner had the shopkeeper returned home than Ibrahim's mother brought him two more eggs, and the shopkeeper took them to the Shah. The Shah allowed him to take as much money as he could lift up from his treasury. Naturally the shopkeeper hastened to take advantage of the Shah's generosity.

Thus in a very short while he became one of the richest men in the town. When she learnt how the shopkeeper had grown rich so quickly, Ibrahim's mother stopped selling him eggs, although he offered her a great deal of money for them.

One day Ibrahim took some eggs and set off to see the Shah. The Shah rewarded him even more generously than the shopkeeper. He permitted him to take as much money as he liked from the royal coffers.

On hearing that Ibrahim had gone to see the Shah, the shopkeeper set off after him. On the way he met Ibrahim coming home and asked him to share the money he had been given. When Ibrahim refused, the shopkeeper flew into a rage and swore to avenge himself.

After this Ibrahim went to the Shah several times with presents and was generously rewarded by him each time.

Meanwhile the envious shopkeeper was wondering how to get hold of Ibrahim's riches and deprive him of the source of his wealth.

One morning the shopkeeper went to the Shah and said:

"O, Haven of Peace! Do not take any more eggs from Ibrahim, but rather ask him for the bird of paradise that lays these beautiful eggs. It is worthy of the Shah, not of some country bumpkin."

The Shah thought for a while and agreed with the shopkeeper.

The next day Ibrahim again brought some eggs to the Shah. The Shah rewarded him as usual and asked him to bring the bird that laid the beautiful eggs. Ibrahim was loath to comply with the Shah's request.

Dispirited he returned home and told his mother what the Shah had ordered. It was a great blow to them to part with the bird of paradise, although they knew the Shah would reward them generously.

Mother and son racked their brains, but could not think of anything. They would have to obey the Shah's orders and let him have the beautiful bird.

Next day Ibrahim took the bird to the Shah. The Shah was so delighted at the sight of it that he allowed Ibrahim to take as much gold as he could carry from the royal treasury.

This made Ibrahim a really rich man. Moreover he became one of the Shah's courtiers and visited him daily.

The shopkeeper was tormented with envy. He could not bear the Shah's affection for Ibrahim. One day he went to the Shah and said:

"O, Haven of Peace! The bird that Ibrahim brought you lays only three eggs a week and will stop laying completely soon because it has no mate. Tell Ibrahim to go and catch a mate for it."

The Shah did as the shopkeeper said and the following day, when Ibrahim came to see him as usual, ordered him to find a mate for the bird forthwith or pay for it with his life.

Heavy of heart Ibrahim went home and told his mother what had happened. His mother comforted him.

"Go back to the place where you caught the bird, my son," she said. "Lay down the net and play your pipe. When a mate appears be sure not to let it escape."

Ibrahim was cheered by his mother's words. He set off once more on his journey. On the third day he came to the edge of the forest. Here again he built himself a hut, spread out his net and began to play his pipe, waiting impatiently, for the beautiful bird to appear.

At last it came, and Ibrahim caught it without much difficulty in his net. The second bird was even more beautiful than the first one. Ibrahim was overjoyed at his good fortune and straightway set off home.

He was so tired by the journey that he slept three days and three nights on his return. On the fourth day he set

off to see the Shah taking the bird with him. The Shah marvelled greatly at the new bird's beauty and again rewarded Ibrahim lavishly.

When he heard of this the shopkeeper flew into a terrible rage. He was even more tormented by envy. He had been hoping to get rid of Ibrahim once and for all, but now Ibrahim had risen even higher in the Shah's favour.

The shopkeeper tried to think of a way of putting an end to Ibrahim and at last resolved to tell the Shah about the magic rose. He who found the rose could enjoy its beauty, freshness and gentle perfume all year round. But finding it was no easy task. It grew in one garden only on a single bush. The garden belonged to a Div, who had already killed many people daring to approach the walls of his garden. His garden was surrounded by walls that were thirty feet high and three feet thick without a single entrance.

Early next morning the shopkeeper went to the Shah who was in fine spirits and received him graciously.

After a short silence the shopkeeper began:

"O, Haven of Peace! You are exceedingly rich and powerful. You receive many guests from different lands and they find one thing only lacking in your palace: you do not possess the magic rose."

"I would gladly reward him who got me this rose," said

the Shah. "But I have heard that many have tried to get it and parted with their lives."

"Your wish is easily carried out," the shopkeeper said. "Ibrahim the orphan, who is now a rich man thanks to your favours, possesses magic powers. It was thanks to these powers that he got you the birds of paradise. For him nothing is impossible."

The Shah believed the shopkeeper and even appointed him chief counsellor for his quickwittedness. Just then Ibrahim appeared, and the Shah bade him do as the shopkeeper had suggested.

Ibrahim had never heard about the rose and did not know where or how to get it.

He went home with tears in his eyes. In vain did his mother question her son about the reason for his bitter tears. Ibrahim could not utter a single word and eventually his mother began to weep with him. They sobbed hard and long, until they went to sleep. When they awoke, however, Ibrahim told his mother about the Shah's new command. The unfortunate woman had heard many times of the magic rose and knew how hard and dangerous it was to get. She was sure her son would never return from this new journey. Yet he must obey and do as the Shah bade him.

In despair Ibrahim wished to set off at once to find the

rose and certain death in order to put an end to his sufferings. But his mother persuaded him to stay a few days more with her.

The poor mother did not let her son out of her sight. She would gladly have renounced all their riches if only her son could stay with her. Each day she thought up all manner of tasty dishes which she prepared in abundance. But Ibrahim's thoughts were not on food. He kept thinking of the journey that lay ahead.

At last the day came, when his mother embraced him for the last time and gave him her blessing for the perils that lay ahead. Ibrahim took plenty of money with him, for the road was a long one.

The tale is quick in the telling, but it was a long time before Ibrahim reached the garden where the magic rose bloomed.

At last in the third year of his wanderings Ibrahim saw from a hilltop the high walls of the mysterious garden in the distance.

He rested on the hill for six days and on the seventh went cautiously up to the garden.

The garden was so big that it took him a whole day to walk round its walls. Yet nowhere in the garden walls did he find an entrance. He was about to lie down and sleep, when he suddenly heard a loud roar. Turning round he saw a monster as big as a mountain advancing towards him. It was the Div, the owner of the garden. Ibrahim was seized with fear and hid behind a bush.

Meanwhile the Div advanced up to the bush, but fortunately did not notice Ibrahim.

Going up to the garden, the Div struck the wall with his fist. The wall parted at once, and the Div went into the garden. In the twinkling of an eye Ibrahim sprang out of his hiding-place and slipped in behind the Div. Entering the garden, he was amazed at its beauty and fragrance. But he did not take his eyes off the Div until the monster entered the palace. Ibrahim dared not follow him for fear that the Div would notice him and tear him to pieces.

Ibrahim sat down under a tree and wondered what to do next. Eventually curiosity got the better of him and he resolved to enter the palace.

He passed through many richly adorned chambers until he came at last to a hall of pink marble where a maiden of exquisite beauty sat on a fine carpet. Next to her with his head in her lap lay the Div. Seeing the strange youth enter, the beautiful maiden took pity on him and made signs begging him to go away, but Ibrahim would not. Then the beautiful maiden said:

"O, unhappy youth! Do you not see this giant? He has just fallen asleep. Tomorrow he will wake up and tear you to pieces. Go now before it is too late."

To this Ibrahim replied that once having seen her he could not leave her captive in the Div's hands. He would take her away with him or die.

"Do not try to free me," the beautiful maiden said. "Many brave men have sought to do this and all have perished, here in the Div's palace. I do not want you to die because of me. Rather tell me what brings you here and perhaps I may be of use to you."

Ibrahim replied that this was the third year of his wanderings and he had come to release her from captivity.

Hearing this, the beautiful maiden removed the Div's head from her lap, rose from the carpet, took Ibrahim into a secret chamber and bade him sleep and rest there until the following day. When the Div woke up and went hunting, as was his custom, they would have time to decide what to do. So saying the beautiful maiden went back to the hall, sat down as before and put the Div's head on her lap.

Next day the Div awoke, twitched his nose and told the beautiful maiden there was a smell of human flesh in the palace.

"Perhaps you tore some wretched human to pieces and

your mouth still smells of him. Otherwise who would dare to enter here?"

The Div believed her and went off hunting. Then the beautiful maiden went to see her guest and found him asleep. She woke Ibrahim up and they resolved to flee together.

The Div had many fleet-footed horses. The beautiful maiden chose the six most spirited and bade Ibrahim saddle them. He did her bidding at once. Then they went to the Div's secret chamber where he kept his gold and filled eight sacks with it, put the sacks on four horses, mounted the other two and set off.

That evening the Div returned from hunting and, not finding his beloved in the palace, he flew into a terrible rage. He searched through all the palace chambers and hunted all round the garden, but in vain. Hurshid, for that was the beautiful maiden's name, had vanished without a trace.

Then the Div rushed to the stables to saddle his favourite fleet-footed horse, but he had vanished too. He leapt onto another horse and tore off in pursuit.

Ibrahim and Hurshid galloped all day without respite. On the following day Hurshid said to Ibrahim:

"Look back and tell me what you see."

Ibrahim replied that he could see a kind of cloud in the distance.

"That is no cloud," Hurshid said. "It is steam pouring out of the Div's jaws and nostrils. He is greatly angered and has set off after us in pursuit."

After a while Ibrahim looked back again. This time he heard a sound like the howling of the wind.

"That is the Div's breath," the beautiful maiden said. "It means he is not far away from us."

Ibrahim looked back a third time and saw that the cloud had drawn close and enveloped them. A light rain began to fall.

"The Div is just behind us," Hurshid explained. "That rain is his saliva."

Then they raced even faster to escape from the Div. After a while Hurshid told Ibrahim happily that now they had nothing to fear for they had crossed the line beyond which the Div could not follow them.

Their swift steeds carried them the rest of the way in two months, and by the third month they were already home. Ibrahim's mother could scarce believe her eyes when she saw her son. Her joy knew no bounds. But Ibrahim did not recognise his pale, wasted mother with the red eyes. She had hardly eaten or drunk since parting with her son and had wept constantly for him.

Ibrahim and Hurshid arrived so tired that it took them

a whole month to recover. Each day Ibrahim became more attached to the beautiful Hurshid, who also loved him deeply. Hurshid had been carried away by the Div eight years ago, when as a little girl she had been out playing with her friends.

At last, when he was rested, Ibrahim began to build a palace for Hurshid that was to excel the Shah's in elegance and beauty. And then they planned to wed.

Two months after their homecoming, Ibrahim suddenly remembered about the magic rose which the Shah had sent him to find. In the Div's palace he had fallen in love with Hurshid so deeply that he had forgotten about the rose and come home without it.

Now he was faced with the choice of setting off once more to find the rose or fleeing with Hurshid to another land. Seeing her future husband's pale, sad face, Hurshid was greatly troubled and asked the cause of his grief. Then Ibrahim confessed to her that he had gone to the Div not in order to free her from captivity, but because the Shah had sent him there for a rose which he had forgotten to bring back.

The beautiful maiden reassured Ibrahim and bade him give her a dish. Then she tapped the tip of her nose with her finger. Straightway two droplets of blood ran out of her nose onto the dish and turned into two bunches of exquisite roses that never faded.

For a long time Ibrahim stood speechless with amazement and delight. Then he seized the roses and hurried to the Shah. The Shah was overjoyed with the roses and rewarded Ibrahim handsomely. But the shopkeeper, who now resided in the Shah's palace, turned livid with anger. He had never expected to see Ibrahim again and had thought him dead.

Once more Ibrahim's fame gave him no rest. He resolved to have Ibrahim sent on a mission that would be impossible for any mortal.

Choosing a suitable moment, the shopkeeper began to speak.

"O, Haven of Peace!" he said. "You have quite forgotten your dear departed parents. Let us send Ibrahim to the hereafter to enquire as to their health and condition."

The Shah thanked the shopkeeper for reminding him about his dear departed parents and vowed to find out at all costs how they were faring in the hereafter.

He summoned Ibrahim, gave him a letter and bade him set off the very next day to the hereafter to deliver the letter to his parents.

Ibrahim was very troubled and would have gladly refused such an unheard-of mission, but the Shah insisted that his order must be obeyed without any excuses.

The unfortunate Ibrahim went home in despair and told

Hurshid of the Shah's command. She reassured him and counselled him thus:

"My dear one! It is clear that your Shah lacks wit and is therefore easily deceived. Go away somewhere for a year, then come back and tell the Shah that his parents are in good health and were pleased to hear from him."

Ibrahim did as Hurshid said, took leave of his mother and his fair beloved and set off on his way.

On he went, how long no one can say, until he came to a big city in another land. Here he spent a year learning to read and write and mastered several foreign tongues.

Meanwhile Hurshid saw to the building of the palace.

A year later Ibrahim returned.

In order to rid himself of his enemy the shopkeeper, Ibrahim thought up a plan. He went to the Shah and said:

"O, Haven of Peace! Your parents are in good health and thank you for remembering them, but they are insulted that you dispatched me, and not your head counsellor, to them. They would have sent you far more tidings if it had been he."

The Shah believed Ibrahim and rewarded him, but the shopkeeper who was present, grew pale with fear when he heard these words. The Shah was so taken with the idea of learning more about his dear departed parents that he resolved to send his head counsellor, the former shopkeeper, to visit them.

A few days later the shopkeeper was ordered by the Shah to go to the hereafter and visit his long departed parents.

The shopkeeper was greatly troubled. He could not refuse, however, for if he did the Shah had threatened to chop off his head. He pondered hard and long what to do and finally resolved to turn to Ibrahim for help.

The following day the shopkeeper went to see Ibrahim, fell down on his knees and begged for help with tears in his eyes, offering him nearly all he possessed. At first Ibrahim refused to help him, but then he told him how to find the shortest way to the hereafter. Taking the shopkeeper to a well a hundred foot deep, he said:

"Jump down this well. At the bottom you will see two paths: one going east, the other going west. If you choose the first, it will take you three years to get to the hereafter, but you will have much suffering. If you choose the second, it will take you five years and you will not feel tired at all."

The stupid and envious man believed Ibrahim, closed his eyes and jumped down the well into his grave. Thus perished the shopkeeper for his greed, spite and envy.

Ibrahim made ready for his wedding.

The Shah waited long for his head counsellor to return,

then finally burst with impatience and himself went to join his parents in the hereafter.

Ibrahim soon married his beautiful Hurshid.

The wedding feast lasted forty days and forty nights. Then Ibrahim and Hurshid settled down to live happily ever after.

THE STORY OF ZARNIYAR WHO HAD ALL HER WITS ABOUT HER

This is a story about a merchant named Mamed who lived in the city of Misar.

One day Mamed bethought him of going off to trade in a distant land. He bought a large number of goods, hired servants and bidding farewell to his family, set out on his way with his caravan.

Having travelled for many months and visited many different places, he came at last to a city he had never heard of before.

Here he decided to rest after his long travels and put up at a caravansary.

As he sat there eating and drinking, a stranger came up to him.

"You must have come from distant parts if you do not know the customs of this city, merchant," the man said.

"And what are the customs of this city?" Mamed asked.

"I'll tell you what they are. Every merchant who comes

here presents a gift to the Shah. In return, the Shah invites the merchant to his palace and plays a game of backgammon with him."

What was Mamed to do? He knew he had to go to the Shah whether he liked to or not. So, choosing the richest silks he had, he laid them out on a golden tray and set off for the palace.

The Shah took the gifts and plied the merchant with questions, asking him where he came from, what goods he traded in and what cities he had visited. Mamed answered him truthfully, and the Shah heard him out and said:

"Come to my palace tonight, and you and I will play backgammon."

It was evening when Mamed came to the palace, and there was the Shah waiting for him, the backgammon board set up before him.

"Hear me out, merchant," said the Shah, "I have a learned cat that can balance seven lighted lamps on its tail for hours on end. If not one of them falls off while we are playing, all your wares will be mine and you will be bound and thrown in a dungeon. But if the cat so much as moves from its place, all the riches in my treasury will be yours and you can do with me whatever you wish."

Mamed sat there listening to the Shah and he cursed himself

silently for ever having come to this city. For he knew that he could not run away, and to protest was out of the question. There was no way out but to do as the Shah said.

"One can easily lose one's life here, let alone one's wares!" thought he.

The Shah now called his learned cat, and the cat came and twirled its tail and sat down in front of him.

"Bring the lamps!" the Shah commanded.

And seven lamps were at once brought in and placed on the cat's tail.

The Shah moved closer to the board, and the game began.

The merchant could not stop himself from glancing at the cat as he played. And the cat sat there as if turned to stone and did not so much as stir.

So a day passed, and a night, and then another two days and two nights, and the game went on. The cat sat there as before.

At last Mamed could bear it no longer.

"I cannot play any more! You win, Shah!" he cried.

That was all the Shah was waiting for. He called his servants and said to them:

"Bring me all of the merchant's wares and all his gold. And as for the merchant himself, bind him and throw him in a dungeon!"

The servants did as the Shah bade, and Mamed found himself in a dungeon. He sat there and he cursed the Shah and his learned cat and himself too for not having had the sense to pass the city by.

But now let us leave Mamed for a while, so that I can tell you about his wife Zarniyar.

Zarniyar was at home where Mamed had left her, waiting patiently for his return, but he did not come and she began worrying about him.

"Perhaps something has happened to him?" thought she.

She had lived with these anxious thoughts for a long time when Mamed's servant, who had gone with him on his travels, appeared at her doorstep. His face was streaked with dirt and his clothes were in tatters.

"Hear me, mistress!" cried he. "The Shah of a faraway land has imprisoned the master and has seized all his goods. I alone of the servants was able to run away and I barely escaped with my life. What are we going to do?"

Zarniyar bade the servant tell her the whole sad story. She heard him out to the end and then ordered a large number of mice to be caught and placed in a chest. When this had been done, she dressed herself in man's clothing, hid her long hair under a high fur cap, and taking a bagful of gold and silver, set off at the head of a caravan to rescue her husband.

She journeyed without halting or delays of any kind and in due time arrived in the city where her husband was.

She bade some of her servants wait at the caravansary for her and the rest go with her to the Shah's palace.

Then, taking a large golden tray, she placed on it many costly gifts, and accompanied by the servants who walked behind her carrying the chest full of mice, set out for the palace.

They neared the palace, and Zarniyar said to the servants:

"I shall be in the Shah's chamber playing backgammon with him, and you must let the mice in through the door one by one."

The servants remained at the door with the chest, and Zarniyar entered the Shah's chamber.

Said she to the Shah:

"Long years to you, O ruler of rulers! I have brought you rich gifts, as is the custom of your country."

Taking her for a man, the Shah welcomed Zarniyar graciously, put the choicest delicacies before her and invited her to join him in a game of backgammon.

"What are your rules, O ruler of rulers?" asked Zarniyar.

Said the Shah:

"We shall play until my learned cat moves from its place. If it does, then I will have lost the game, and you shall do with me whatever you wish."

"Very well," said Zarniyar. "Let it be as you say."

The Shah called his learned cat, and the cat padded in and sat down very solemnly in front of him. Then the Shah's servants appeared, bringing seven lamps which they placed on the cat's tail.

The game began, the Shah smiling as he played and only waiting for the young merchant to admit himself the loser.

Some time passed, and Zarniyar's servants opened the chest and let a mouse into the Shah's chamber.

When the cat saw the mouse its eyes began to glitter and it made as if to move from its place. But the Shah looked at it so sternly that it quietened at once and seemed frozen to the spot.

In a little while Zarniyar's servants let several more mice into the chamber. The mice began running up and down the floor and scuttling about near the walls. Now, this was too much for the cat, learned though it was. It gave a miaow, and jumping up suddenly, whereupon all the seven lamps dropped to the floor, began chasing the mice. And shout as the Shah might, it would not listen to him.

Then only did Zarniyar call her servants, who rushed into the room, bound the Shah hand and foot and began belabouring him with leather thongs. And they would not stop even when he called for mercy.

"I will let out all my captives and give back to them all I took away, only spare me!" the Shah cried.

But Zarniyar's servants went on whipping him. And though his people heard the Shah's cries they would not come to his aid, for all had long grown weary of his cruelty and greed.

Zarniyar then freed her husband and all who were with him and had the Shah thrown into the dungeon.

After that Zarniyar and Mamed returned to their native city of Misar and lived there in peace and happiness.

The Georgian tale, *The Poor Man and the Knight's Three Pomegranates,* has been illustrated by the Moscow artist, Natalia Nesterova, who has won awards at major exhibitions in Moscow, Japan, the German Federal Republic and the Netherlands. Her paintings are to be found in the Tretyakov Gallery in Moscow and the Russian Museum in Leningrad.

People's Artist of the Georgian Soviet Socialist Republic Tengiz Samsonidze has won prizes at many major Republican and All-Union book design competitions, and also at international exhibitions in the German Democratic Republic, Poland and Yugoslavia.

His best known paintings are *Georgians with Peter the Great, Morning, Rustavi* and *Motifs of Old Tiflis.* In this book he has done the drawings for the Georgian tale *The Fair Maid From Faraway Nigozeti.*

Felix Giulanian, chief artist at the Armenian publishing house of Sovietakan Grokh, has illustrated the folk tale *Azaran Bulbul.* Giulanian has illustrated many other books for both children and adults, some of which have won awards at Republican and All-Union book design exhibitions.

The creative range of Togrul Narimanbekov, People's Artist of the Azerbaijan Soviet Socialist Republic, is very broad indeed, including painting, drawing, stage design and monumental art.

His work has been exhibited in the German Federal Republic, the United States, Canada, the German Democratic Republic, France, Hungary, Italy, Syria, the United Arab Republic and Cuba.

The artist's canvases may be found in the Tretyakov Gallery in Moscow, the Russian Museum in Leningrad, the Oriental Arts Museum in Moscow, the collection of Professor P. Ludwig in the German Federal Republic and the Azerbaijan Arts Museum in Baku.

In this book Narimanbekov has illustrated the two Azerbajan tales entitled *The Story of Zarniyar Who Had All Her Wits About Her* and *Ibrahim the Orphan and the Greedy Shopkeeper.*

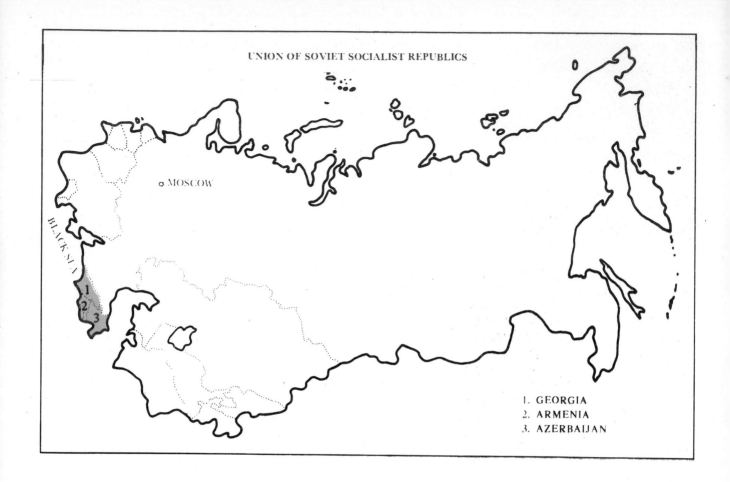

MOSCOW

BLACK SEA

1. GEORGIA
2. ARMENIA
3. AZERBAIJAN

The Caucasian republics of Georgia, Armenia and Azerbaijan became part of the Soviet Union shortly after the Great October Socialist Revolution of 1917. These ancient peoples already had a long history and a very distinct cultures of their own by the time they joined together with the Russian people.

As independent republics Georgia, Armenia and Azerbaijan retain their national traditions. In recent decades these republics have produced much of interest in almost all spheres of activity. Their peoples never forget their history. They take pride in the splendid monuments of their ancient cultures that are a source of inspiration in painting, architecture, music and literature.

Historically the Caucasian peoples share much in common, but it is the specifically national features of each of these peoples reflected in the various spheres of folklore that have inspired the creation of operas and ballets, paintings, majestic sculpture and immortal poems.

Such literary masterpieces as the poem "David of Sasun" based on the Armenian heroic epos, the Georgian epos about Amirani and the Azerbaijani tales and legends about wise, strong heroes are united by a single theme, the fight for self-determination and freedom, the theme of self-sacrifice for the happiness of one's fellow-countrymen.

Every nation's culture is rooted in folklore. One branch of folklore, the popular oral tradition, is of historical significance, because it is into legends, fables and folk tales that the common people weave their aspirations, their joy and sorrow, their hopes and beliefs. The days of mighty princes and cruel shahs, the traditional characters of folk tales, are now a thing of the past, of course, but writers and scholars who love their native land and know its history endeavour to recreate the past for their readers and to extol the names of its fine and fearless heroes. They collect and record folk poems, tales and songs which are then carefully studied and published in new editions of folklore collections. Altogether this represents a vast amount of material that has been assembled over many decades. This book introduces the reader to a few of the most characteristic national features in the tales of the Caucasian peoples.

REQUEST TO READERS

Raduga Publishers would be glad to have your opinion of this book, its translation and design and any suggestions you may have for future publications.

Please send all your comments to 17, Zubovsky Boulevard, Moscow, USSR.

Сказки народов Закавказья
СКАЗКИ НАРОДОВ СССР

На английском языке

© Состав, иллюстрации, аппарат. Издательство "Радуга", 1986г.

Printed in the Union of Soviet Socialist Republics

6.75